- T
- Save o
- New Tax

1988 Quick Reference Guide to the TAX REFORM ACT

Longman Financial Services Publishing
a division of Longman Financial Services Institute, Inc.

Introduction

This booklet is intended to assist you in your 1987 year-end tax planning while you still have time to take steps that could significantly reduce your overall tax liability. However, its usefulness does not end on December 31, 1987. We have designed it to assist in your planning for the coming year also.

This is a transition year in the implementation of the Tax Reform Act of 1986, which substantially overhauled our tax system. For most purposes, the 1986 Tax Act will be fully implemented in 1988. Therefore, decisions you make now will have broad implications for many of the investing and purchasing strategies you use over the next several years.

In addition to the suggested tax strategies in this book, we have included in the Appendix income tax rate tables for both 1987 and 1988. Also included is a section on checking how much Social Security has been credited to your account, which should be done every few years.

Contents

Compensation and Employee Benefits

Minimizing 1988 Taxes

Appendix

Preliminary Considerations

The ideas discussed in this booklet are based on tax rules in effect on October 1, 1987. During 1987 the old tax rules and the new rules created by the Tax Reform Act of 1986 are in transition. For the most part, the following provisions will be fully implemented in 1988:

- Individual rates will be lower — in some instances as much as 27% lower. (See the rate tables on pages 42 and 43.) In 1987 there are five brackets, with rates varying from 11% to 38.5%. In 1988, rates will be compressed into two brackets: 15% and 28%. An additional 5% tax will apply to certain high-income taxpayers.

- In 1987, long-term capital gains are taxed as ordinary income, with a maximum rate of 28%. In 1988 capital gains will also be treated as ordinary income, and therefore can be taxed at rates as high as 33% if you are subject to the additional 5% surtax.

- In 1987 you will still be able to use 65% of your tax shelter losses to offset income from salary and investments, provided these losses stem from investments made before October 23, 1986. In 1988 only 40% of these losses may be used to offset salary and investment income, and by 1991 you will not be able to use these losses at all to offset this income.

- Starting this year, the alternative minimum tax (AMT) could play an increasingly important role in tax planning strategies. As the top tax rate drops from 38.5% to 28%, you may inadvertently fall into the complex AMT system with its 21% flat tax rate for individuals. (This trap is even more formidable for corporations.)

Although the 1986 Tax Act made major changes in the tax law, many planning techniques that were used effectively in the past remain valid. Furthermore, other planning techniques that had fallen out of general usage (e.g., private foundations) have been revitalized by the rate reductions.

Tax Strategies for Individuals

Deferring income and accelerating deductions — usually good tax planning strategies — will prove particularly valuable during the rest of 1987, especially in light of lower tax rates in 1988. But a word of caution: If you have tax credits or net operating loss carryovers that will expire if unused in 1987, or if you are in an alternative minimum tax posture for 1987, you may benefit from accelerating additional income into 1987 to take advantage of these circumstances. (The AMT is discussed beginning on page 21.)

Following are some specific suggestions regarding income and deductions for 1987 and 1988 in light of the 1986 Tax Act.

Deferring 1987 Income to 1988

Year-End Bonuses. Maximum 1988 tax rates will be at least 14% lower than 1987 rates, and this makes it attractive to defer 1987 bonuses until some later year. To make it effective, however, you must decide to defer the bonus income to a later year *before* performing the services giving rise to the income.

Certificates of Deposit. The purchase of certain short-term (one year or less) certificates of deposit at this time by cash-basis individuals will defer the reporting of 1987 accrued interest income until your *1988* tax return is filed — April 17, 1989 at the earliest. The CD must be the type that pays no interest without substantial penalty before the 1988 maturity date. Treasury Bills and U.S. Savings Bonds offer a similar opportunity for deferral because T-Bill and Savings Bond interest generally is not recognized as income until the investment is redeemed. Note also that T-Bill and Savings Bond interest is not subject to state or local income tax.

Installment Sales. If you plan to sell nonpublicly traded property in 1987, you may be able to use the installment sales method. This method generally allows you to spread the reporting of any gain over the period the proceeds are received. Thus, a provision in the sales contract deferring part or all of the purchase price for a few months into 1988 may result in income tax deferral on part or all of your gain for a full year (in addition, you will take advantage of the lower tax rates for 1988). However, you may be required to recapture previously taken depreciation *in the year of sale,* not as payments are received. Thus, unless you have sufficient cash from other sources to pay any additional taxes, you should structure the installment sale of any personal property so that it provides you with sufficient cash by the due date of your return to pay the tax on the recapture.

Finally, more complex rules apply if you sell real property used in a trade or business or held for rental, and the sales price exceeds $150,000.

Accelerating 1987 Deductions

Cash basis taxpayers can exercise a fair amount of control over the timing of deductions. A check you deliver or mail during 1987 generally qualifies as a payment in 1987, even if the check is not cashed or charged against your account until 1988. Furthermore, payments of medical expenses and charitable contributions by credit card are deductible when the charge is made, rather than when you pay the credit card bill.

State and Local Taxes. You may want to pay in December of 1987 those state and local taxes that have accrued (property, estimated income, etc.) that you would normally pay in the first part of 1988. This generally will allow you to accelerate your Federal tax deduction a full year. Further, you will receive the benefit of a deduction while the higher 1987 tax rates are in effect.

Personal (Consumer) Interest. Although the 1986 Tax Act is phasing out this deduction, 65% of your personal interest expense is still deductible for 1987. However, over the next four years the itemized deduction for personal interest you incur on credit card balances, car loans, and other personal indebtedness will be fully phased out. You may want to consider decreasing balances on high-interest credit cards and paying off other nonmortgage loans whenever possible.

Home Mortgage Interest. "Qualified mortgage interest" — interest on loans secured by your principal residence or on a second home equal to the original purchase price of the residences plus the cost of any home improvements (or fair market, if lower) — is generally fully deductible. Interest on the loan balance that exceeds this limit is not "qualified mortgage interest" unless the mortgage was taken out before August 17, 1986 or the proceeds were used for certain medical or educational purposes.

If you have significant personal interest deductions, consider converting the expense into "qualified mortgage interest" through a home equity loan, thus potentially bypassing the phase-out of the personal interest deduction. However, you should be aware of a potential trap relating to mortgage refinancings. If you become liable for the AMT, interest on a refinanced mortgage may not be entirely deductible for AMT purposes.

This would be the case if the interest on the refinanced debt were attributable to a loan balance exceeding the amount of the outstanding loan *before* it was refinanced.

Investment Interest. Generally, to the extent of investment income, you can deduct interest incurred on indebtedness to purchase an investment. However, you cannot deduct interest on debt used to finance the purchase of tax-exempt securities. For years before 1987, you could also deduct $10,000 of investment interest expense in excess of your net investment income. However, for 1987, only 65% of the $10,000 allowance is deductible. Over the next four years, the full $10,000 allowance will be phased out.

Medical Expenses. A medical deduction can be taken only if your medical outlays exceed 7.5% of your adjusted gross income (AGI). To exceed this threshold, you may have to bunch expenses into a single year (by accelerating or deferring payment, as appropriate). In this regard, remember that a divorced parent generally can deduct medical payments incurred for his or her child even though the other parent claims the dependency exemption.

Health Insurance Costs of Self-Employed. Beginning in 1987, self-employed individuals may deduct as a business expense 25% of the amount paid to purchase medical care insurance for themselves, their spouses, and their dependents. The deducted amount cannot be used in determining whether a self-employed individual has reached the 7.5% medical expense threshold; however, the 75% not deducted from business income can be taken into account for purposes of the itemized medical expense deduction.

Often-Overlooked Deductions and Credits

- Your costs for *stock that becomes worthless* are deductible (generally as a capital loss) in the year it becomes worthless; but you may need a professional appraiser's report or other evidence to prove the stock has no value.

- If you incur expenses for the *care of certain dependents* or an incapacitated spouse so you can work or look for employment, you can take a *tax credit* of up to 30% of the work-related expenses. Work-related expenses are limited to $2,400 for one qualifying individual and $4,800 for more than one qualifying individual. Qualifying individuals include dependents under the age of 15 and physically or mentally incapacitated dependents or spouse.

- You may be able to claim deductions for the business use of a portion of your home if (1) it is *exclusively* used on a *regular* basis either as a principal place of business or as a place to meet customers, clients, or patients or (2) the business portion of the home constitutes a separate structure. However, the deductions attributable to qualifying business use are limited to the gross income from the activity, reduced by interest and taxes related to the business portion of the home, and further reduced by all other non-home office deductible expenses related to the business activity. Deductions disallowed solely because of the income limitation may be carried forward to later years.

- *Travel expenses,* including food and lodging, incurred primarily to inspect or maintain investment properties are deductible. However, only 80% of the expenses for food or meals may be deducted.

Beginning in 1987, certain miscellaneous itemized deductions are deductible only to the extent they exceed 2% of your adjusted gross income.

Nevertheless, one or more of the following deductible items may represent a sizable payment and put you above the 2% threshold for other miscellaneous deductions.

- *Legal expenses* for certain tax planning and for negotiating employment contracts. If you are affected, instruct your attorney to itemize the bill, indicating the amount attributable to *tax planning* incident to a divorce, estate planning, or drafting an employment contract.
- *Tax return preparation* fees.
- *Professional dues and publications.*
- *Safe deposit box fees,* to the extent the box is used to store investments, such as stocks and bonds.
- *Automobile expenses.* Use actual figures rather than the IRS per-mile allowance. Studies have shown the actual cost to operate an automobile may be more than twice the current per-mile allowance. The allowance is 22.5 cents a mile for the first 15,000 business miles per year and 11 cents a mile thereafter. It is 12 cents a mile for charitable use.
- *Business gifts* up to $25 per recipient.
- Expenses for telephone, postage, office supplies, and publications related to investment activities or to the determination of your tax liability.
- *Educational expenses* related to business, to the extent they neither qualify you for a new job nor enable you to meet the minimum entry-level educational requirements for your employment.
- *Fees to employment agencies* to help you find a job may also be deductible.

Tax Considerations of Investing

This section is intended to help you evaluate the tax impact of investment strategies. However, tax is only one factor in making an investment decision, and you should evaluate all considerations — including the following — before formulating your year-end investment strategy.

Tax-Exempt Investments. The 1986 Tax Act may be an incentive for you to look more closely at adding state or local government bonds to your investments. Even though you may have to pay state or local taxes on income from obligations of other than the taxing state, tax-exempt bonds are virtually the last refuge from Federal income taxation. Moreover, you can purchase tax-exempts with a relatively small investment by investing in a tax-exempt bond fund.

To determine whether to invest in tax-exempt securities, compare the net after-tax income from a tax-exempt investment with a comparable taxable investment. The following table shows — according to various tax brackets — the yield required on a taxable investment to result in the same net after-tax income as a tax-exempt investment. You can determine your *Federal* income tax bracket by referring to the rate tables in the Appendix.

Equivalent Investment Yields

Your Tax Bracket	*6%*	*7%*	*8%*	*9%*	*10%*	*11%*
15%	7.06	8.24	9.41	10.59	11.76	12.94
28%	8.33	9.72	11.11	12.50	13.89	15.28
33%	8.96	10.45	11.94	13.43	14.93	16.42

If you are in the 28% bracket, for example, a tax-exempt investment with an 8% yield would provide you with the same after-tax dollars as a taxable investment with an 11.11% yield.

Note: Tax-exempt bonds also have some drawbacks: Interest on funds borrowed to purchase tax-exempt securities is not deductible. Beginning in 1987, some tax-exempt interest is considered a preference item for the AMT.

Timing of Security Transactions. You can generate tax losses for 1987 by selling "losers" as late as December 31. The 1986 Tax Act eliminated installment reporting for sales of stocks, securities, and other property traded on an established securities market. Thus, gain realized on these properties must be reported in the year of sale (determined by the trade date) even though the settlement date falls in the next year. The character (long- or short-term) and the amount of gain or loss are determined at the trade date, not the settlement date.

You also can act at any time this year to nail down gain on a security transaction and defer the tax effect until next year. This can be done by selling short in 1987 securities that you already own, but not closing the short sale until 1988. This is known as a *short sale against the box.*

Year-End Strategies. While market and individual circumstances may dictate different action, the trading position you are in as the year end approaches will determine the strategy you should follow to reduce your Federal income taxes. For example, if a tally of your trading results to date shows you are in a net capital gain position, consider recognizing capital losses to offset this gain. If you are in a net capital loss position, you will be able to offset up to $3,000 of ordinary income. You should consider recognizing additional capital losses up to the limit. If your net capital losses exceed the $3,000 limit, consider recognizing additional capital gains to absorb the excess instead of carrying the losses over to future years.

Wash Sales. If you believe a security you are holding is a good long-term investment despite a current downturn in its value, and you want to realize your loss for 1987, exercise care if you plan to reestablish your position following the sale. The tax law disallows a deduction for a loss from a wash sale of securities. A wash sale occurs if you sell securities at a loss and within 30 days before or after that sale you purchase the same or substantially identical securities. The wash sale rules also apply to short sales. Keep in mind that the wash sale rules do not apply to securities sold at a gain. In fact, under certain circumstances, you may want to recognize a capital gain and then reestablish your position to obtain a stepped-up basis in the security. See your tax advisor for details.

Family Tax Planning

Family tax planning will now require considerably more effort to realize tax benefits. Following is a brief summary of the steps you can still take to minimize Federal income taxes in connection with your family financial planning.

Middle- and upper-income taxpayers have traditionally realized significant tax savings by shifting taxable income to lower-tax-bracket family members. However, the 1986 Tax Act virtually eliminated the benefit of using reversionary trusts — such as Clifford and spousal remainder trusts — to accomplish this end.

Beginning in 1987, attaining age 14 becomes a milestone for tax purposes. Children 14 or older will be taxed at their own — presumably lower — tax rates on their investment income, rather than at their parents' top marginal rate, which is the case for children under 14. The following discussion analyzes family tax planning strategies in light of the different tax treatment for investment income earned by children under 14 and those 14 or older.

Children under 14 — No Current Taxable Income. For children under 14, unearned income, i.e., from investments, over $1,000 is taxed at the parents' tax rate unless the child is in a higher bracket. The effect of this new rule can be diminished if the child, or a trust of which the child is a beneficiary, acquires investments producing little or no current taxable income. Such investments include tax-deferred annuities, municipal bonds, Series EE Savings Bonds, and growth stocks. In addition high-risk investments, such as limited partnership interests, gems, art, coins, and bullion, also may not produce income until they are sold.

Children under 14 — Earned Income. Although children are not allowed a personal exemption if they are claimed as dependents on the parents' tax return, a child who has earned income is entitled to the standard deduction ($2,450 in 1987 and $3,000 in 1988) and the IRA deduction ($2,000). Thus, you can employ your child in the family business, and he or she can earn up to $4,540 in 1987 ($5,000 in 1988) without incurring any tax liability. If the family business is a sole proprietorship and the child is under 21, Social Security taxes can also be avoided.

Children 14 Years or Older — Gifts of Appreciated Property. Using the tax rates in effect in 1988, up to $17,850 of income of a child 14 or older is taxed at a 15% rate, while his or her parents will generally be taxed at a 28% rate. Therefore, a 14-year-old child's income can be increased (and the parent's tax liability reduced) if the parent gives apprcciated property to the child. The parent has no income on the gift, and when the child sells the property, the gain will be taxed at the child's presumably lower tax rate. Further, the income from reinvesting the proceeds of the sale is taxed at the child's lower tax rate.

Social Security Numbers for Dependents

Along with the reduced tax rates, the 1986 Tax Act added new compliance rules. If you claim exemptions for dependents — for example, a child or grandchild — on your tax return, starting with your 1987 return (generally due April 15, 1988) and later, you must provide the Internal Revenue Service with the Social Security numbers of dependents who are or will be five years old or older before the end of the tax year. Failure to do so may subject you to a penalty.

While the 1987 filing period seems a long way off, remember that it takes time to get a Social Security number. If a person you expect to claim as a dependent on your return does not have a Social Security number, you or that person should apply for one as soon as possible. You can obtain Form SS-5 for this purpose from the IRS, the Social Security Administration, or your tax advisor.

Estimated Taxes

An individual who fails to make a quarterly estimated tax payment equal to one-fourth of the "required annual payment" can be subject to a penalty. The "required annual payment" is the lowest of the following three safe harbors: (1) 90% of the tax shown on the return for the current taxable year; (2) 100% of the prior year's tax; or (3) 90% of the tax that would be due if income actually received by the end of a quarter were annualized. The penalty is based on the difference between each required installment and the amount paid for the period of the underpayment.

Use Withholding Rules to Your Advantage

As you near the end of the year, you may find the estimated tax payments you made have not been enough to prevent underpayment penalties. If you are an employee, increased withholding may be the answer to this shortfall. Unlike estimated tax payments, which are credited when paid, withholding is treated as having been received in equal installments throughout the year. An increase now in your withholding may be treated as though one quarter of the increase were paid in each installment period. There is no tax detriment to an employer who accommodates such a request.

Charitable Giving

Charitable Contributions. If you plan to make substantial contributions in the next few years, you should consider making them this year, *unless* your tax rate will increase in 1988. Tax benefits from your contributions will be the greatest in the year your tax rates are highest. You might even consider borrowing to make some contributions. The tax savings may more than offset the partially or wholly nondeductible interest expense of a short-term loan. Remember that a contribution made by credit card is deductible when charged to your account (not when the bill is paid). However, only those who itemize deductions can take a deduction for contributions.

You should also consider using appreciated property to make charitable contributions. You receive an income tax deduction equal to the fair market value of the contributed property without paying tax on the appreciation. However, beware if you are subject to the alternative minimum tax.

Private Charitable Foundation. A private charitable foundation is an organization through which an individual can make charitable contributions. Its creation and funding may be a very useful tax-saving tool. Lower individual tax rates next year give a charitable contribution deduction greater value in 1987, making this year a good year to establish a private foundation. For example, a $10,000 charitable deduction could reduce Federal income taxes by as much as $3,850 in 1987 (38.5% top rate); but in 1988, the $10,000 deduction can reduce taxes by only $2,800 (28% top stated rate).

Private foundations are subject to operational limits, but these restrictions do not pose a significant problem in most situations. Furthermore, some public charities, such as community trusts, may offer an alternative designated fund to achieve similar benefits.

Charitable Lead Trusts. This kind of trust results in a current deduction for the *present value* of the income to be paid by the trust to the charity in later years. To determine the amount of the current charitable contribution deduction, the IRS uses tables, discounting amounts to be received in future years at a specified percentage per year, currently 10%.

Charitable Remainder Trusts. Basically, this type of trust provides that the trust property will be distributed to charity at the end of the trust term, with the grantor (or other beneficiaries) retaining (or receiving) an income interest during the trust term. The amount of the charitable deduction is determined by deducting the present value of the income interest — using the 10% prescribed rate — from the value of the property placed in trust.

Gift and Estate Planning

If you plan to establish a gift program, you may want to start before year end to maximize the annual exclusion of $10,000 per donee ($20,000 if married and your spouse consents). By making qualifying gifts before year end, those amounts can be given now, again in 1988, and then in subsequent years, without incurring a gift tax. Of course, in designing your property-transfer program, you should keep in mind that the maximum gift and estate tax rate is 55% for gifts made and individuals dying in 1987. This rate goes down to 50% in 1988.

Tax Strategies for Businesses

Timing of Income and Deductions

A major year-end business consideration is the timing of income and deductions. Most individuals and many owners of service businesses use the cash method of accounting for tax purposes; however, most other businesses use the accrual method of accounting.

A business's choice of accounting method can substantially affect tax planning. Under the cash method, income or expense items are reported when actually or constructively received or disbursed. Under the accrual method, the right to receive and the liability to pay generally determines when those items are reported. However, for tax purposes, an accrual method taxpayer generally may not deduct a liability before economic performance occurs, i.e., before goods or services are provided.

The use of the cash method of accounting is available, however, to farming businesses, certain personal service corporations, S corporations, and small businesses. All other corporations, partnerships that have a corporation as a partner, tax shelters, and certain tax-exempt trusts must use the accrual rather than the cash method of accounting.

Like individual taxpayers, the typical business will want to defer income and accelerate expenses. Since corporate and individual tax rates will be lower in 1988 than they are in 1987, the following advice is particularly sound:

- Delay deliveries on sales (but consider the potential property tax effect).
- Make sales on consignment or approval (thus delaying billing and payment).
- Make the maximum deductible charitable contributions (up to 10% of taxable income for corporations).
- Contribute the maximum deductible amount to tax-qualified retirement plans.
- To the extent possible, place depreciable property in service before the end of 1987.

The imposition of the 20% AMT for corporations means that corporations must plan with both AMT and the regular tax in mind. (A more detailed discussion of the AMT can be found on page 21.)

Depreciation and Expensing for Business Equipment

Depreciation. The new tax law substantially modified the rules for depreciating property used in a trade or business. The new method, called modified accelerated cost recovery system (ACRS), is generally mandatory for all types of eligible property unless a special election is made to use an alternative method. Eligible property includes all types of tangible property (both real and personal). Modified ACRS, like ACRS under prior law, requires you to recover the cost of qualifying property over a specified number of years. Modified ACRS differs from ACRS in that the recovery periods have been extended for most property. This extension requires you to write off an asset over a longer period.

Starting in 1987, *when* new property is placed in service can have a significant effect on the amount of your depreciation deduction in 1987. Generally, personal property is treated as having been placed in service at the beginning of the third quarter

(July 1 for calendar-year taxpayers) regardless of when it was actually purchased and placed in service. However, if *more* than 40% of the property purchased during the tax year is placed in service during the last quarter of the year, then *all* of the property purchased and placed in service throughout the year will be treated as being placed in service in the middle of the quarter in which it was purchased. Thus, if you are not careful, you may reduce this year's depreciation deductions on property you have already purchased.

Expensing. Under certain circumstances, you can deduct up to $10,000 of an asset's cost in the year it is purchased and placed in service rather than depreciating it over a specified number of years. To qualify for expensing, the asset must be tangible personal property used in an active trade or business. If the asset qualifies, you can expense up to $10,000 in the year it is placed in service.

However, the $10,000 ceiling is reduced dollar for dollar by the cost of the property (otherwise qualifying for the deduction) in excess of $200,000 that you place in service during a year. Other restrictions also apply.

Should You Be Using an S Corporation?

If you now own or may be forming a closely held corporation, you should evaluate the potential tax-saving opportunities of an S corporation. Eliminating double taxation remains the major S corporation benefit, but the 1986 Tax Act gives you more reasons to consider making an S election for your corporation.

Generally, an S corporation is just like any other corporation: it has a "perpetual" life; its management is centralized; its shares can be transferred; and its shareholders are afforded limited liability from creditors. However, for tax purposes, an S corporation is treated somewhat like a partnership. For example, an S corporation, like a partnership, passes its income (or loss) directly through to its owners, so its income generally escapes the double taxation that would be paid by a regular corporation.

Tax Reform and S Corporations. The tax benefits of operating as an S corporation received a big boost from the 1986 tax reform legislation.

- *Tax Rates.* Beginning in 1987, the top individual tax rates are lower than the top corporate rates. As the chart below indicates, the lower individual rates provide an incentive to operate a closely held corporation as an S corporation.

Top Marginal Rate (Calendar Year)

	1986	*1987*	*1988*
Corporations	46.0%	40.0%	34.0%
Individuals	50.0%	38.5%	28.0%
Relative Tax Benefit (Cost)	(4.0%)	1.5%	6.0%

Even in 1988, when an additional 5% tax applies to certain high-income individuals, the top corporate rate will still be higher, and the tax advantage of operating a business as an S corporation will still apply.

- *Penalty Taxes.* S corporations are exempt from the corporate AMT (discussed on page 21), the environmental (Superfund) tax, the personal holding company tax, and the accumulated earnings tax.

- *Estate and Gift Planning.* With the lower individual and corporate tax rates, the estate tax is now the highest tax that some individuals may face (50% after 1987). An S corporation can play an important role in achieving estate planning objectives and minimizing potential estate taxes. For example, control of the S corporation can be passed on to a younger generation by transferring stock to them while the first generation is still active in the business's daily affairs.

In addition, gifts of income-producing S corporation stock to children over age 13, who are taxed on income at their own (presumably lower) rates offer the opportunity to significantly reduce a family's taxes.

- *Cash Method.* S corporations are not automatically prevented from using the cash method of accounting, but regular C corporations are.
- *Passive Income.* The new passive activity rules are intended to restrict tax shelter losses by limiting the deduction of "passive losses." However, S corporations may be a source of passive income to offset passive losses that would otherwise not be usable because of the new limitations. For example, if a shareholder does not materially participate in the trade or business conducted by the S corporation, or if the S corporation is engaged in *any* rental activity, the shareholder's passed-through income is considered to be passive. Passive losses from tax shelters can generally be used to offset only passive income, *not* salary or investment income. Passive losses can be used to absorb income from the S corporation.

To form an S corporation, you must satisfy certain requirements:

- Up to 35 shareholders are permitted (a husband and wife are treated as one shareholder).
- Only individuals, estates, and certain trusts can own stock in an S corporation.

- Only one class of stock is permitted, but the voting rights within the class can differ and the stock may include shares with no voting rights.
- An S corporation may not have active subsidiaries.

State Tax Planning for S Corporations. The Federal tax benefits noted above have prompted many companies to consider an S corporation. However, the state tax side of a proposed election under Subchapter S should also be considered. The states vary in their treatment of S corporations. Some states recognize S corporation status but require a separate state election or additional qualifications. A number of states do not recognize S corporations and tax the company like a regular corporation. Because of the disparity in treatment at the state level, the use of an S corporation may provide significant opportunities to save taxes, but also creates a number of pitfalls, including situations in which the combined shareholder and corporate taxes are significantly higher than the tax burden of a regular corporation. The lesson to be learned: planning for the S corporation election should consider state as well as Federal tax consequences.

Some Drawbacks. Fringe benefits for more-than-2% owner-employees present a drawback to using an S corporation. The limitations for participation in such benefits as group insurance are more restrictive than for owner-employees in regular corporations.

In addition, you should be aware of certain consequences of converting an existing corporation to an S corporation. A tax may apply to the gain ("built-in gain") that has accumulated on corporate assets before the S election when these assets are sold, otherwise disposed of, or distributed to shareholders.

Certain regular corporations worth less than $10 million that convert to S corporations before 1989 may find some relief from the built-in gains tax. Your tax advisor will be able to determine whether you qualify for this special provision. Also, converting to an S corporation carries other associated expenses. For example, a regular corporation will probably have to pay for an appraisal to determine the amount of built-in gain for each asset, such as uncollected accounts receivable and inventory.

Caution: The Alternative Minimum Tax

Tax reduction strategies for your regular tax may not result in the anticipated savings if you are subject to the new alternative minimum tax (AMT). In 1987 corporations will be subject to the AMT, and many more individuals than before will find they owe more tax than the Form 1040 Tax Tables indicate. If you can reasonably estimate your tax position and you anticipate an AMT liability in 1987 or 1988, certain strategies are available to help lessen its impact.

Structure of the Tax

The AMT's fundamental goal is to prevent individuals and corporations with substantial economic income from using preferential deductions, exclusions, and credits to eliminate their tax liability. To achieve this goal, the AMT is structured as a separate tax system with its own allowable deductions and credit limitations. The tax is imposed at a rate of 21% on individuals and 20% on corporations. It is an alternative tax because after computing both your regular tax and AMT liabilities, you pay the higher of the two.

Calculating AMT. The first step in computing the AMT is to determine the income base, known as alternative minimum taxable income, or AMTI. This is done by taking your taxable income, increasing it by preference amounts, and making certain other specified adjustments.

Generally, the required adjustments are intended to convert preferential deductions allowed for regular tax (e.g., accelerated depreciation on real estate) into alternative deductions that are allowable under the parallel AMT system. For example, real property that may be depreciated for regular tax purposes over either 27½ years or 31½ years must be depreciated over 40 years for the AMT. Other adjustments to taxable income must be made by corporations and individuals that use the installment sale method for reporting sales of inventory and certain other property, or that use the long-term contract method of accounting. Net operating losses allowable for the regular tax must also be adjusted for the AMT.

Following are some of the more significant items individuals must add to taxable income in computing AMTI:

- State and local income and property taxes claimed.
- Any miscellaneous itemized deductions allowed.
- Any investment interest expense or personal interest that is deductible under the regular tax phase-in rules.
- Passive losses deductible under the phase-in rules (which allow 65% of such losses in 1987 and 40% in 1988).

Moreover, individuals who exercise incentive stock options must include in AMTI the excess of the fair market value of the stock received over the price paid for the stock. Thus, if you live in a state with high income and property taxes, have large tax shelter investments, large auto loans, or exercise incentive stock options, you are a prime candidate for the AMT.

Individuals and corporations must also add the following preference amounts to their taxable income:

- The excess of a charitable contribution deduction over the adjusted basis of contributed property.
- Percentage depletion claimed in excess of adjusted basis.
- Intangible drilling costs in excess of 65% of net income from oil, gas, and geothermal properties.
- Tax-exempt interest on certain private activity bonds issued after August 7, 1986, reduced by any related interest expense disallowed for regular tax purposes.

Corporations (other than S corporations) must also increase AMTI by 50% of the excess of their adjusted net book income over AMTI computed before this adjustment and without any net operating loss otherwise allowable for AMT purposes. Therefore, differences between book income and AMTI are taxed at an effective 10% rate (50% times the 20% corporate AMT rate).

Corporations and married individuals filing jointly can take an exemption of $40,000 less 25% of AMTI over $150,000. Thus, joint filers and corporations with AMTI of $310,000 or more receive no exemption. Single individuals may take a $30,000 exemption less 25% of AMTI over $112,500.

The applicable AMT rate of 20% or 21% is applied to AMTI net of any allowable exemption. The result (after reduction by any AMT foreign tax credit) is compared to the regular tax (net of the foreign tax credit). Any excess is your AMT, which you must pay in addition to your regular tax.

Determining AMT Exposure

In planning for the AMT, you must first anticipate whether you will be subject to it in either 1987 or 1988. Here are some general rules of thumb:

- Corporations with taxable income over $335,000 will be subject to AMT for calendar year 1987 if AMTI exceeds 200% (40% regular tax rate divided by 20% AMT rate) of taxable income. The ratio is 170% in 1988 (34% divided by 20%).
- Married taxpayers filing jointly are subject to AMT in 1987 only if AMTI is at least 159% of taxable income. As taxable income rises from $200,000, the ratio will approach 183% (1987 maximum rate of 38.5% divided by AMT rate of 21%). For 1988, if taxable income is over $232,500, AMTI must exceed 133% (28% regular tax rate divided by 21% AMT rate) of taxable income. At lower income levels, you must have an even higher ratio of AMTI to taxable income to owe AMT in 1988.

Planning with the Minimum Tax Credit

Whenever you owe the AMT, you will be allowed a "minimum tax credit" to the extent that your AMT is attributable to "deferral" or "timing" preferences and adjustments. An example of a "deferral" preference is accelerated depreciation. Under the AMT, you depreciate real estate over 40 years. Under the regular tax you may depreciate real estate over as few as 27½ years. In both cases you receive the same total benefits of depreciation, but under AMT some of the benefit is deferred 12½ years.

The AMT creates no minimum tax credit that is attributable to "exclusion" items. These items are regular tax deductions or exclusions for which no AMT deduction will *ever* be allowed. For example, itemized deductions — such as state and local taxes, which are not allowable for AMT purposes — are exclusion items. Other exclusion items for individuals and corporations are the preferences for depletion, tax-exempt interest, and charitable contributions of appreciated property.

The minimum tax credit can be carried over to a later year and used to reduce your regular tax in years when you are not subject to the AMT. Thus, the importance of the minimum tax credit is that it converts the AMT from an additional out-of-pocket tax to a tax that, to the extent generated by deferral items, is merely a prepayment of the regular tax.

Planning Strategies — Shifting Income and Deductions

Once you have determined that you are likely to owe AMT for 1987 or any other particular year(s), your next step is to focus on the types of items giving rise to the tax. The proper strategy will depend on whether the AMT is attributable to deferral items, exclusion items, or a mixture of both. These strategies apply both to individuals and corporations, although their different regular tax and AMT rates will affect the amount of tax savings.

If you expect to owe AMT in 1987 with only deferral items, and switch to owing regular tax in 1988, you should use traditional regular tax planning strategies. Income should be deferred to 1988, and/or deductions should be accelerated into 1987. You will benefit both from the drop in regular tax rates in 1988 and from a deferral of AMT that would have been paid in 1987. Accelerating preference deductions into 1987 (e.g., by paying additional state income tax) will not produce *immediate* tax savings, but it will save overall tax because a larger minimum tax credit will be created at 1987's higher regular tax rates. This larger credit may be used to reduce regular tax for 1986 and later years.

If you will have only exclusion items and expect to owe AMT in 1987 and regular tax in 1988, use the reverse strategy to obtain permanent tax savings. Accelerate income from 1988 into 1987 (or defer deductions) to have the income taxed at the AMT rate of 20% or 21% (rather than the higher regular tax rate in 1988). However, income should only be accelerated so that your regular tax will equal your AMT for 1987.

If you have both deferral and exclusion items, proper planning becomes more complex. See your tax advisor for details.

Finally, if you expect to owe regular tax in 1987 and AMT in 1988, you should follow general regular tax planning techniques and accelerate deductions — if possible, preference deductions — into 1987 or defer income to 1988. For example, by moving a $1,000 exclusion item into 1987, you may obtain a $385 immediate tax savings from a deduction that in a 1988 AMT year would produce no tax savings.

Compensation and Employee Benefits

Nonqualified Deferred Compensation

Some employers offer executives the opportunity to defer part of their current compensation to a later date under nonqualified deferred compensation plans. The 1986 Tax Act has made these arrangements even more attractive. To take advantage of the tax rate reduction scheduled after

1987, taxpayers should consider deferring expected income until 1988 or later. If certain requirements are met, the executives will not be taxed on the deferred compensation until it is received. Thus, high-tax-bracket executives in such companies can defer part of their compensation to years when they may be in lower tax brackets (possibly after retirement).

Compensation deferrals could help offset new limitations on elective deferrals under 401(k) plans and the loss of deductible contributions to IRAs. However, because you may defer only *unearned* income, you should enter into a written agreement with your employer to defer the income before it has been earned.

If your employer is a tax-exempt organization, new restrictions generally limit the amount of income that you may defer. Similar restrictions apply if your employer is a state or local government.

Individual Retirement Accounts (IRAs)

The 1986 Tax Act restricted the ability of many taxpayers to make up to $2,000 of deductible IRA contributions ($2,250 if your spouse has no compensation or elects to be treated as having no compensation). In general, your right to make a *deductible* IRA contribution is limited if either you or your spouse:

- Are *eligible* to participate in a qualified defined benefit pension plan.
- Receive an allocation of contributions or employee forfeitures under a qualified defined contribution plan or annuity program.
- Participate in any governmental retirement plan or program other than Social Security.

The limitation on the IRA deduction is phased in gradually. Generally you lose $1 of deduction for each $5 of your income that exceeds the following amounts:

Filing Status	*Phase-Out Begins*	*Deductions Totally Phase Out*
Single* and Heads of Household	$25,000	$35,000
Married Filing Jointly	$40,000	$50,000
Married Filing Separately	—0—	$10,000

*You are considered single, even though legally married, if you file a separate return and live apart from your spouse at all times during the taxable year.

However, to the extent these restrictions apply, nondeductible IRA contributions are permissible. Whether or not deductible, you can make 1987 contributions only up to the unextended due date of your individual tax return (e.g., April 15, 1988).

Your decision to make nondeductible IRA contributions should consider the following factors:

- While earnings on nondeductible contributions are tax-deferred until distributed, a portion of any distribution of such contributions or earnings before age 59½ is subject to a 10% additional income tax, generally a larger portion than the portion that would be subject to penalty if after-tax contributions were withdrawn from a tax-qualified plan.

- Tax-exempt investments offer tax deferral on earnings without the additional income tax on premature withdrawals.

- Certain insurance products offer tax deferral features without withdrawal penalties.

401(k) Plans

If you currently maintain a qualified retirement plan, the above restrictions may prevent your employees from making deductible IRA contributions. A 401(k) plan may allow your employees to replace their lost IRA deductions.

A 401(k) plan is a feature of a profit sharing or stock bonus plan under which an employee can elect to have a portion of his or her salary contributed to the plan. These so-called elective contributions, which can be made throughout the year through salary reduction or at year end through bonus deferral, are excluded from the employee's income until distributed. You can add a 401(k) feature to an existing plan, or you can adopt a new plan at any time. However, an employee must make the election to reduce salary or bonus before the salary or bonus is earned.

Tax-exempt organizations and small employers may be able to provide this same benefit to employees under a 403(b) annuity plan or simplified employee pension (SEP), respectively. An employee's total elective contributions under all plans in which he or she participates are limited to $7,000 a year. This $7,000 annual limit is increased to $9,500 for elective contributions made to a 403(b) annuity plan.

Keogh (HR 10) Plans

A Keogh (HR 10) plan is a special plan for self-employed taxpayers and any of their employees. If you have already established one, you can deduct from your 1987 income those contributions made *any time before* the extended due date of your 1987 income tax return. Contributions to partnership Keogh plans must be made before the partnership return is due.

Under either a profit sharing Keogh or a money purchase Keogh for 1987, a self-employed individual can deduct contributions up to approximately 13.04% or 20%, respectively, of net earnings from self-employment, with an overall limit of $30,000 on contributions to all such plans.

In contrast, a defined benefit Keogh plan requires actuarially determined amounts to be contributed each year. This type of plan may allow for greater deductible contributions, depending on your age. The maximum annual benefit you may fund under a defined benefit Keogh is limited to the lesser of $90,000 or 100% of your average earnings from self-employment (determined net of your contributions to the Keogh plan) for your highest three consecutive years of earnings from a particular trade or business. These limits are reduced for early retirement before the Social Security retirement age and for less than 10 years of participation in the plan. Contributions are deductible to the extent necessary to fund plan benefits but not to the extent that they exceed self-employment income for the year.

Generally, anyone with self-employment income may establish a Keogh plan, even if the individual also earns income as an employee. For example, corporate director fees and consulting fees generally constitute self-employment income. Beware that recent IRS regulations would generally prohibit "inside" directors (directors who are also employees of the corporation on whose board they sit) from establishing or continuing a Keogh for director fees from that corporation. Also, additional restrictions may apply to more-than-5% owners of certain service corporations. Otherwise, you can contribute to a Keogh plan from self-employment income regardless of whether you participate in an unrelated employer's qualified plan.

Accelerating Tax Deductions

As a general rule, a company can claim a tax deduction, at *1987* rates, for contributions made to its qualified retirement plans through the extended due date of the company's Federal income tax return, provided the contributions are treated by the plan as 1987 contributions. Given the scheduled decline in tax rates for 1988, this ability provides an incentive for maximizing your 1987 contributions.

If your company maintains a defined benefit pension plan that allows contributions to range between a minimum and maximum amount, the company should consider contributing the maximum amount for 1987. This not only maximizes deductions in a high-tax-rate year, it may allow for reduced future funding obligations. And, if your company normally makes monthly contributions to such a plan, you may be entitled to deduct up to 21 months of contributions at 1987 tax rates without making additional contributions.

Qualified Plan Distributions

The Internal Revenue Code now penalizes qualified plan and IRA distributions that are too early, too late, or too high. For instance, distributions received before age 59½ are generally subject to a 10% additional income tax. On the other end, distributions are generally required to commence once you attain age 70½. If at that time certain minimum distribution requirements are violated, the government imposes a penalty equal to 50% of the amount of the shortfall (effective for qualified plan distributions after 1988). However, you are also penalized if you receive your retirement benefits too quickly. A new 15% excise tax is imposed on excess annual distributions from all qualified plans and IRAs. A distribution is "excess" to the extent it exceeds $150,000 ($750,000 for a separate lump sum distribution). This excise tax becomes a 15% additional estate tax should you still have excess total retirement benefits accumulated at the time of your death. And to complicate matters further, you will need to decide whether to elect to have certain of your retirement benefits "protected" from these 15% penalties before you file your 1988 tax return. So retirement planning becomes even more important than in the past.

Lump Sum Distributions. Generally, a qualifying lump sum distribution received by a plan participant may be rolled over tax-free, within 60 days of receipt, to another qualified retirement plan or IRA. Alternatively, a participant can elect to be taxed currently on such a distribution. Individuals who have attained age 59½ may make a one-time election to claim 5-year forward averaging. Regardless of age, individuals can elect to treat any pre-1974 portion of the distribution as capital gains for purposes of offsetting capital losses. (Capital gains are no longer subject to a favorable tax rate.) Capital gains treatment is phased out beginning in 1988.

Under a special grandfather rule, individuals who attained age 50 before January 1, 1986, may, regardless of age, make a one-time election to claim capital gains treatment (at a special 20% tax rate and without regard to the phase-out) and either 10-year forward averaging (at 1986 tax rates) or 5-year forward averaging (at the then-current tax rates). Generally, you will be better off using 5-year averaging once the amount of your lump sum distributions received during the year exceeds $375,000. However, other factors may enter into your decision to be taxed currently.

Minimum Plan Distributions. If you retired or reached age 70½ before 1987 and have not yet taken a distribution from your IRA or qualified retirement plan, you may need to take up to 3 years' worth of distributions by December 31, 1987. Failure to take the minimum IRA distribution could trigger a 50% penalty on the shortfall, while failure to take the minimum qualified plan distribution could jeopardize the plan's tax-qualified status. Even if you have been taking distributions, you may not have been taking enough. The IRS has only recently issued guidance in this complex area. Because the penalties are extreme, it would be prudent to consult your tax advisor.

Cash Tight? Consider Pension Funding Waiver

Employers maintaining certain types of qualified plans are subject to minimum funding requirements. Missing a contribution or making a late payment can subject an employer to penalty taxes that can be substantial. However, these penalty taxes may be avoided.

An employer needing to conserve cash can ask the IRS to waive its annual contribution for a particular year. Alternatively, minor alterations of the plan's actuarial assumptions often result in drastic reductions of required funding obligations.

Deductibility of Employee Medical Expenses

The U.S. Supreme Court decided in 1987 that an accrual basis taxpayer that reimburses its employees for medical expenses on a pay-as-you-go basis may not deduct medical expenses incurred during the year until claims for reimbursement are received. If your company has been accruing expenses for incurred but not reported medical expenses, you need to change your method of accounting to comply with this decision. Also, you should consider establishing a funded welfare benefit plan (e.g., a voluntary employees' beneficiary association, which is tax-exempt under Sec. 501(c)(9)), to continue to accelerate a deduction for this item.

Planning for the Coming Year

The close of the year is always a good time for employers to reexamine their employee benefits programs. However, in 1987 year-end planning has special significance — it should usher in a full year of analysis and plan design aimed at coping with the many employee benefits provisions of the 1986 Tax Act that become effective in 1989.

The following rules are among the key provisions that apply to qualified retirement plans for plan years beginning *after 1988:*

- The rate at which an employee's employer-provided retirement benefit must become nonforfeitable is accelerated. A plan will have to satisfy either a five-year or a seven-year schedule.
- Each plan must cover the fewer of 50 employees or 40% of includible employees.
- New coverage rules will require a plan to cover a broader cross-section of eligible employees.
- Defined benefit and defined contribution plans that tie benefits to Social Security payments will generally have to reduce the disparity between those benefits provided above and below the so-called "integration level."
- Minimum distributions will have to commence for any employee by the April 1 following the calendar year in which the employee attains age 70½.
- The funds available for a hardship withdrawal from a qualified 401(k) cash or deferred arrangement will be limited to an employee's actual elective contributions (i.e., amounts that the employee contributed).

- A 401(k) plan will not be able to condition any plan benefits, other than matching employer contributions, on an employee's elective contributions.

For tax-exempt employers, the following restrictions will apply to 403(b) tax-sheltered annuities after 1988.

- Amounts attributable to elective contributions will be available for distribution only upon death, disability, separation from service, attainment of age 59½, or financial hardship. Hardship withdrawals will be allowed only from actual elective contributions.
- Employer contributions other than elective contributions will be subject to the same coverage and nondiscrimination rules as qualified plans.
- The opportunity to make elective contributions will generally have to be available to all employees.

Finally, for plan years beginning after 1988 (or plan years beginning three months after applicable regulations are issued, if earlier), employer-maintained accident or health plans, group-term life insurance plans — and, possibly, group legal services plans, educational assistance programs, and dependent care assistance plans — will face an incredibly complicated new set of qualification and nondiscrimination rules. Benefits provided under cafeteria plans will also be subject to these rules.

Although plans generally do not have to be amended for the above provisions until the last day of the first plan year beginning after 1988, they must operate in accordance with each provision as of the first day each provision becomes effective. Because these provisions are complex and, in many cases, will require radical changes in plan operation and design, it is essential that employers begin grappling with them now to ensure timely compliance later.

Minimizing 1988 Taxes

Your income tax planning should not be limited to one year; you can begin now to plan your tax strategies and decisions for 1988 and later. Develop your tax strategies to take advantage of the tax law changes discussed below.

Individuals

The most noteworthy change in the tax law for individuals in 1988 is the full compression of tax rates into just two brackets: 15% and 28%. However, this fully phased-in rate reduction is accompanied by an additional tax of 5% on taxable income falling within certain ranges, designed to phase out the benefit of the 15% bracket and personal exemptions of higher-income taxpayers. Beginning in 1988, tax rates will be among the lowest they have ever been. Too many individuals overlook this fact and instead focus only on the phase-outs of the 15% bracket and the personal exemptions for higher-income taxpayers. Don't be so concerned by phase-outs that you miss an opportunity presented by lower rates.

Remember: The 5% surtax notwithstanding, tax rates will not drop below the 15% and 28% rates applicable in 1988. In fact, Congress is talking about *raising* individual income tax rates again to solve Federal budgetary shortfalls. In light of this possible increase, 1988 may be an excellent year to recognize income rather than planning to defer it to 1989 and future years, when income tax rates may be higher. You should apply this same restraint and reason to other phase-outs scheduled for the next few years.

Interest Deduction Strategies. The 1986 tax law repealed the deduction for consumer (or personal) interest expense — but over five years. That means for 1987, 65% and for 1988, 40% of such interest is still deductible. The deductible portion declines to 20% in 1989 and 10% in 1990; in 1991 the deduction is completely phased out.

One planning strategy to consider involves reducing your personal interest expense. Generally, you can do this by using your own resources (including home equity loans) for personal expenses, borrowing when necessary to finance your investments or business assets. However, do a tax cost-benefit analysis before rushing out to liquidate investments to pay off consumer debt.

In light of the four-year phase-out of this deduction, you may be better off settling for a percentage of the deduction rather than eliminating a favorable return on investment funds. Furthermore, in most situations it will never be advantageous to pull money out of a tax-deferred vehicle — such as your employer's profit sharing plan — to retire consumer interest — even if you are entitled to no interest deduction (i.e., in 1991 and later years). Your share of a qualified plan or other tax-deferred arrangement earns money tax-free until you withdraw it, so the balance is almost always in favor of leaving your share within the plan unless you must withdraw it, especially considering the possibility of penalty taxes upon withdrawal.

Keep in mind that interest on indebtedness to purchase *business assets* is completely deductible. However, interest on indebtedness used to purchase investments, while deductible, is subject to the investment interest expense limitation. *Qualified mortgage interest* also remains fully deductible (see page 4) and provides some opportunity for tax planning. For example, a highly leveraged purchase of a "second residence" for your college student's use while in school will provide you with a full deduction for interest and taxes while giving you the opportunity to realize substantial capital appreciation.

Passive Loss Strategies. Similar to the rules for the personal interest expense phase-out are those applying to your deductions for *net* losses generated by investments in passive activities, such as limited partnership tax shelters. Deductions for net losses generated by passive activities are generally allowed only to the extent that you have net income from these passive activities. However, keep in mind that losses from some passive activities are phased out at the same rate as personal interest. If you held a passive activity on October 22, 1986 (the date President Reagan signed the tax bill into law) or acquired it under a binding contract entered into on or before that date, 65% of your net loss is deductible for 1987, 40% in 1988, 20% in 1989, 10% in 1990. Your net losses from pre-October 23, 1986 passive activities will be entirely nondeductible by 1991.

However, unlike disallowed personal interest expense, any net losses disallowed under the phase-out rule for these passive losses can be used to offset net passive income in future years. If you have significant amounts of currently nondeductible net passive losses you may also want to consider disposing of some of your passive activities. But be aware that many interests in passive activities, such as limited partnership tax shelters, are selling at deep discounts because of the passive loss restrictions. You may benefit from retaining such passive interests and offsetting any losses by investing in "PIGs," passive income generators, i.e., any passive activity that generates income, not losses.

Alternative Minimum Tax. The lowering of the top marginal rate increases the possibility that many individual taxpayers will face the AMT for the first time. At greatest risk are high-income taxpayers who previously received regular tax benefits from investments in tax shelters, and those subject to a phase-out of their AMT exemption. Specific items that may trigger the onset of the AMT (without giving rise to a credit available for use against future years regular tax liability) include any itemized deductions not allowable for AMT purposes, any portion of a charitable contribution of property attributable to untaxed appreciation, and certain tax-exempt interest. Your tax advisor can help you determine whether you are subject to the AMT.

Businesses

A number of tax saving opportunities available to businesses in 1988 are scheduled to expire on or before January 1, 1989. Also, discussions on Capitol Hill point to a general need for more tax revenues. Simplest among the revenue-raising options proposed thus far is an increase in the corporate tax rate. As of July 1, 1987, the 34% corporate income tax rate was fully implemented. Therefore, in anticipation of a possible increase, corporations, like individuals, should take advantage of that rate to the greatest extent possible in 1988.

Among the items set to expire after 1988 are the small business exception to the repeal of the *General Utilities* doctrine for liquidating corporations, the targeted jobs tax credit, the research and development credit, and the eligibility of certain "transition" property for ACRS depreciation and investment tax credit. You should ask your tax advisor to explain how you may be able to take advantage of these soon-to-be eliminated opportunities for tax saving.

Appendix

Tips on Filling Out Your W-4

By now, you have probably seen — and made your best efforts to fill out — the highly publicized withholding forms required by the 1986 Tax Act. Your employer uses these forms to determine your tax liability for withholding tax purposes.

You should have completed a W-4 (or "short-form" W-4A) and returned it to your employer by September 30, 1987. If you have not, do so immediately. If you failed to supply your employer with a Form W-4 or W-4A by the deadline, your employer is required to withhold taxes as though you claimed only one exemption (if single) or two (if married). Your employer will continue withholding on this basis until you complete a W-4 or W-4A indicating your correct withholding allowances.

If you have completed a new withholding form, you can still change your withholding at any time. In addition, if you change jobs, your new employer will ask you to complete another W-4 or W-4A.

Here are some tips to keep in mind if you will be filling out a new withholding form:

- Claim all the withholding allowances to which you are entitled. But keep in mind that if you claim more than 10 allowances, your employer will be required to send copies of your W-4 to the IRS. The IRS may ask you to verify that you are in fact entitled to the allowances you claimed. You could also be subject to penalties if the IRS determines that you claimed too many allowances without having a reasonable basis for doing so.

- Determine whether you are entitled to the "special withholding allowance." If you are, claim it; otherwise too much tax will be withheld from your pay. For example, you could be entitled to the special allowance if you are married, have only one job at a time, and your spouse does not work. There are other justifications for the special allowance. Check with your tax advisor.
- You may *want* extra tax withheld from your pay if you have significant nonwage income for which tax is not withheld, such as interest, dividends, and other investment income.

How to Request a Social Security Statement of Account

Social Security benefits are based on government records of your earnings. The process is automated, but it is not uncommon for errors to creep into the system. These errors could be difficult to correct when you want to collect your benefits.

However, you can verify your earnings record conveniently and at only the cost of a postage stamp. Call or write your local Social Security Administration (SSA) office and ask for a "Request for Statement of Earnings." Complete the form and send it to the SSA, which will send you a report of your earnings, with the most recent three years individually identified. For prior years, an aggregate sum will be shown. You can compare the record against the information on your W-2 forms.

Because the period within which mistakes are easily corrected is limited (generally three years, three months, and 15 days), you should request an earnings record every three years.

1987 Federal Income Tax Rates

*Tax Rates**	*Joint Returns*	*Heads of Households*
11%	0-$3,000	0-$2,500
15%	3,001-28,000	2,501-23,000
28%	28,001-45,000	23,001-38,000
35%	45,001-90,000	38,001-80,000
38.5%	Above 90,000	Above 80,000

*Tax Rates**	*Single Individuals*	*Married Filing Separately*
11%	0-$1,800	0-$1,500
15%	1,801-16,800	1,501-14,000
28%	16,801-27,000	14,001-22,500
35%	27,001-54,000	22,501-45,000
38.5%	Above 54,000	Above 45,000

*Tax Rates**	*Estates and Trusts*
11%	0-$500
15%	501-4,700
28%	4,701-7,550
35%	7,551-15,150
38.5%	Above 15,150

Corporations
Blended Rates for Calendar-Year Corporations

Rates	*Taxable Income*
15%	0-$25,000
16.5%	25,001-50,000
27.5%	50,001-75,000
37.0%	75,001-100,000
42.5%	100,001-335,000
40.0%	335,001-1,000,000
42.5%	1,000,001-1,405,000
40.0%	Above 1,405,000

*Long-term capital gains are taxed at ordinary income tax rates, subject to a maximum rate of 28%.

1988 Federal Income Tax Rates

Tax Rates	*Joint Returns*	*Heads of Households*
15%	0-$29,750	0-$23,900
28%	29,751-71,900	23,901-61,650
33%	71,901-149,250	61,651-123,790
28%	Above 149,250[a]	Above 123,790[b]

[a]Plus the lesser of 28% of allowable personal exemptions or 5% of taxable income in excess of $149,250.

[b]Plus the lesser of 28% of allowable personal exemptions or 5% of taxable income in excess of $123,790.

Tax Rates	*Single Individuals*	*Married Filing Separately*
15%	0-$17,850	0-$14,875
28%	17,851-43,150	14,876-35,950
33%	43,151-89,560	35,951-113,300
28%	Above 89,560[c]	Above 113,300[d]

[c]Plus the lesser of 28% of allowable personal exemptions or 5% of taxable income in excess of $89,560.

[d]Plus the lesser of 28% of allowable personal exemptions or 5% of taxable income in excess of $113,300.

Tax Rates	*Estates and Trusts*
15%	0-$5,000
28%	5,001-13,000
33%	13,001-26,000
28%	Above 26,000

Corporations

Rates	*Taxable Income*
15%	0-$50,000
25%	50,001-75,000
34%	75,001-100,000
39%	100,001-335,000
34%	Above 335,000